NATIONAL GEOGRAPHIC KiDS

FUNNY
Animals

HA HA HA!

CRITTER COMEDIANS,

PUNNY PETS, and

HILARIOUS HIJINKS

This is *TOAD-ALLY* silly.

NATIONAL GEOGRAPHIC
WASHINGTON, D.C.

EVEN DOGS HAVE
RUFF DAYS!

OOOH,
I ate one too
many doggy
treats...

The giraffe laughed at the terrific traffic.

CRITTER COMEDIANS
Fuzzberta the Guinea Pig

EXCUSE US, have you seen this guinea pig? She's a master of disguise; she could be anywhere. Is she playing a game of football? Or lounging on the beach? Or is she over behind that dinosaur? WAIT— that's no dino, that's Fuzzberta!

Fuzzberta is a rescued guinea pig who has attracted a fan following for her adorable disguises and costumes. Her owner, "Monica the human," loves to snap the glamorous guinea pig in all kinds of silly scenarios—running from monsters, fighting dragons, going dogsledding, or even dressed as Albert Einstein! Monica and Fuzzberta aim to spread happiness with their fantastic photos.

When she's not in disguise, Fuzzberta loves snacking on strawberries or hanging out with her guinea pig pals: MiniGuineaPig, Jennifuzz, Billy Blob, Jelly Baby, and Shnoopy. But who knows where Fuzzberta will appear next—or what she'll appear as!

MiniGuineaPig

Fuzzberta and her friends are all advocates for **ANIMAL ADOPTION.**

Guinea pigs aren't pigs, but may have gotten their name from their **SQUEALING NOISES.**

Fuzzberta shows her smarts by dressing as Albert Einstein.

It's called *FASHION*, dear. Look it up.

9

HIPPOS TWIRL POOP

WHAT DO MOST PEOPLE FIND ROMANTIC? Is it flowers and chocolates? Not for hippopotamuses. No, for hippos, the height of romance is ... flinging poop.

Ooh-la-la!

Most times, two bulls, or male hippos, turn their bodies parallel, with their heads in opposite directions, and swing their tails rapidly to shower their excrement for several feet in all directions. They can create a perimeter of poop up to 60 feet (18 m) in diameter!

Male hippos use this bizarre behavior to mark their territory and—believe it or not—to attract a mate. Female hippos tend to choose mates with larger territories, so a particularly large splatter of poop is just as nice as a big old bouquet is to us humans.

This behavior also unintentionally serves a larger purpose: Hippo dung is important for the environment. It provides their habitat with a ton—pun intended— of nutrients.

So go on, hippos, let your feces fly!

A male hippo uses his tail to fling waste.

Hippos secrete a natural **SKIN MOISTENER** and sunblock.

I'll take breakfast *IN BED* today!

My dog is so naughty that:

His trainer **RETIRED** after his obedience class.

All our shoes are now just **"SHOE."**

The neighbors **BOUGHT US** a pooper-scooper.

Even our cat can't **IGNORE** him.

Everyone now thinks my little **BROTHER** is an **ANGEL.**

We have to take him for walks in a giant **HAMSTER BALL.**

13

ANIMAL:

Gentoo penguin

NAME:

Rick the Referee

FAVORITE SPORT:

Anything with a black-and-white ball!

FAVORITE SAYING:

"What's black and white and red all over? Me, giving out a red card!"

Dog Runs Half Marathon

JUST IMAGINE: You're running a marathon. The wind is in your hair, your feet are pounding the pavement, and you're almost finished! You're so close—you just have to pass a runner on your left, and then that dog on your right ... wait, what?

In the town of Elkmont, Alabama, U.S.A., a bloodhound named Ludivine joined in on a fund-raiser half marathon. Ludivine had been let out to do her business but snuck out of her yard and made her way to the racecourse—all without her owner knowing! She joined the rest of the runners, quickly charmed her competitors ... and raced past them.

RACE YA!

The hilarious hound ran the entire 13.1 miles (21 km) and managed to finish in seventh place. She even received a medal! And best of all, Ludivine's doggy dash caught the attention of several newspapers, bringing tons of attention to the fund-raiser.

In fact, the organizers of the marathon even changed its name—it is now called the Hound Dog Half Marathon. Good job, Ludivine—that's doggone great!

A bloodhound can follow a **SCENT** for more than 130 miles (209 km).

According to legend, the very **FIRST MARATHON** occurred more than 2,500 years ago!

This nap certainly has my *SEAL* of approval!

ANIMAL:

Chihuahua

NAME:

Bobbi the Beachgoer

FAVORITE ACTIVITY:

Sunbathing

FAVORITE SAYING:

"Go *in* the water?

No way. I'd get my outfit wet!"

21

Waffles shows his wild side in a stylish lion costume.

CRITTER
COMEDIANS
Waffles the Cat

WAFFLES—JUST FOR BREAKFAST, YOU SAY? Don't be silly! Waffles the cat knows that waffles can be eaten at any time. They can even be worn.

However, Waffles' life didn't start out so golden and fluffy. Waffles needed a home, but no one would adopt him. Apparently, people thought his unique looks made him "ugly." Luckily, one couple knew that this was nonsense. What they didn't know was that bringing Waffles home would completely change their lives!

The couple loved to snap pictures of Waffles, and they were surprised to find that those pictures were gaining attention—especially one picture of Waffles wearing a slice of bread around his head. Of course, it's hardly surprising—who doesn't love Waffles? Now this cool cat is living a syrupy-sweet life, posing for funny pictures—including, of course, with waffles—and delighting fans.

And best of all? Waffles can be taken to go. This globe-trotting star travels in a special cat backpack, or even in a baby carrier. How sweet!

Waffles is listed as one of the **TOP PET INFLUENCERS** in the world.

23

The **sloth** could see the **moth** with glee.

24

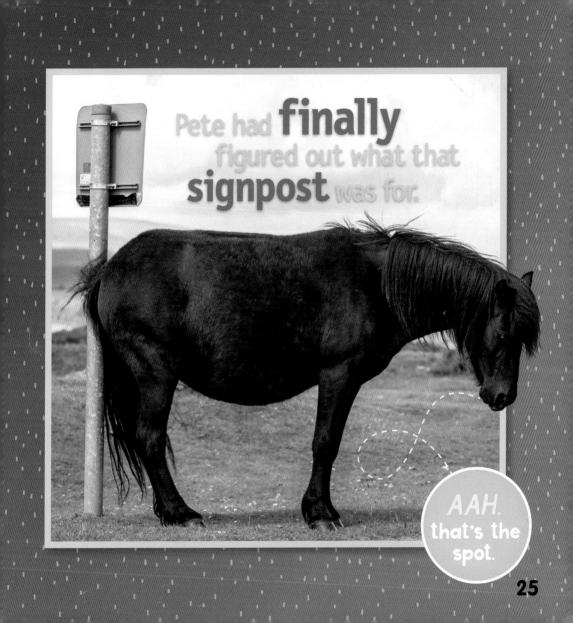

Pete had **finally** figured out what that **signpost** was for.

AAH. that's the spot.

DANCING FERRETS

Everybody
DANCE NOW!

IMAGINE YOU'RE VISITING a friend's home to see their new pet ferret. You don't know much about ferrets and think they're cute, but so far you've only ever seen them in pictures.

Soon though, the ferret is sauntering around on its hind legs with its tail fully puffed up, playfully hopping and swaying to and fro, and blowing your mind in the process.

"How did this ferret learn to belly dance?" you wonder. "Is this behavior normal, or am I watching a bona fide circus act?"

In fact, this is fairly common behavior for ferrets. Known as the "weasel war dance," this combination of wiggling and hopping originated in the wild. The eye-popping movements are thought to help the wild relatives of ferrets, such as weasels, confuse and disorient their prey and even help them escape predators. For the domesticated ferret, though, this special jiggle and wiggle just means that the ferret is happy and excited to play. Some ferrets will even start boogying to convince their human companions to join in on the fun.

So the next time you see a ferret hopping and bopping, get your groove on! Who knows—maybe the weasel war dance will be the next big dance craze.

A **GROUP OF FERRETS** is called a **BUSINESS.**

Ferrets secrete an oil that gives them a **MUSKLIKE** odor.

27

28

I'm king of the mountain— er, tree!

29

Llamas were domesticated around **5,000** YEARS AGO.

LLAMAS are related to camels.

Leaping Llama

CASPA WAS A GRUMPY LLAMA. He was fluffy and cute, sure, but he definitely wasn't cuddly. In fact, as soon as the two-year-old llama arrived at Black Rock Llama Center in Cheshire, Wales, all he seemed to do was spit, kick, and nip at unguarded ankles. He also refused to go near his owner, Sue Williams, instead playing elaborate games of tag that sometimes lasted days! Sue refused to give up, though, and decided to give the silly llama a different game to play: She set up an agility course, similar to the kind dogs use, and led Caspa through it. Success! Over a short period, Caspa reached new heights—literally. He went from grumpy llama to leaping llama, regularly clearing hurdles more than 3 feet (1 m) tall. In fact the frisky flier even broke a world record: At an agility show, he cleared a jump of 3 feet 8.5 inches (1.13 m). And as hilarious as it may be to see a llama soar, the real victory was Caspa's transformation from grump to lovable leaper.

Llamas **SPIT** when they are irritated.

You humans might think you're cool with your earbuds, but I've got *EARBIRDS!*

These are some *TWEET* BEATS!

My cat is so lazy that:

He lets **MICE** share his food bowl.

He takes real **BATHS** instead of giving himself a bath.

He takes a nap to recover from **SLEEPING** all night.

He gets **MANICURES** instead of using the scratching post.

The neighborhood dogs think he's a **STUFFED ANIMAL.**

SHRIMP SHOWDOWN

WATCH OUT, SEA LIFE—there's a new sheriff in Shrimptown.

Snapping shrimp—sometimes called pistol shrimp—might seem a little, well, shrimpy. The pint-size pinchers are no bigger than the size of your finger, but don't be fooled—these crustaceans pack a serious punch. Snapping shrimp have their very own built-in weapon: a single enlarged claw that they use to shoot underwater "bullets" at prey.

If you've ever dreamed of an underwater Old Western showdown, then get ready to be delighted. When a snapping shrimp draws air and water into its claw, it creates a bubble. By snapping the claw closed, the shrimp can send this "bubble bullet" flying at its opponent at up to 62 miles an hour (100 km/h)—almost as fast as a cheetah can run. That's what we call a quick draw!

Once the shrimp has hit its prey, it doesn't need a lasso to collect dinner. That's because the prey has been stunned by the force of the bubble. So, do you still want to say "Howdy" to this rough-and-tumble sharpshooter? No thanks!

If a shrimp feels threatened, it can **SHED ITS CLAW** to escape, and later regrow it.

REACH
FOR THE
SKY!

The
sound of the
**"BUBBLE
BULLET"**
bursting can
be heard by
humans.

SHERIFF

The temperature
within the bubbles
can reach more than
8000°F
(4427°C)!

ANIMAL:

English bulldog

NAME:

Bullzo the Clown

FAVORITE ACTIVITY:

Clowning around

FAVORITE SAYING:

"We used to do my act with biscuits

... until I ate 'em all!"

Birds
of a feather
OWL-WAYS
flock
together.

Petite Pig Gets Big

WHEN STEVE JENKINS ADOPTED ESTHER, he was excited to welcome a miniature pig into the family. Often called micro-pigs, miniature pigs average between 100 and 150 pounds (45–68 kg)—that's about six <u>times</u> smaller than an average oinker. Steve hadn't been expecting to own a pig, but Esther needed a home, and surely a micro-pig wouldn't get in the way ... right?

Well, a micro-pig might not get in the way, but it turns out that Esther was no miniature oinker! She began to grow ... and grow ... and grow, right up to a sizable 600 pounds (272 kg)! Steve and his partner, Derek Walter, were shocked but saw that enormous Esther was something special. Sure, she made massive messes, but she also had a humongous heart. Steve and Derek made a decision: They would buy a farm and open the Happily Ever Esther Farm Sanctuary to care for Esther and other animals in need.

These days, Esther is still huge—in more ways than one. She has tons of adoring fans on social media and has made a huge impact for other needy animals. This supposedly petite porker became a huge star!

Esther has her own **BEST-SELLING** book.

BABY
PIGS
are sometimes
called shoats.

39

Toad *STOOL?* More like frog umbrella.

I'M READY FOR MY CLOSE-UP!

A mountain lion can **JUMP** as far as 40–45 feet (12–14 m).

A remote wildlife camera in the Hollywood Hills snapped this picture of P-22.

CRITTER
COMEDIANS
P-22

IN HOLLYWOOD, one celeb-kitty is the cat's meow! Meet P-22, the mountain lion unexpectedly *cat*apulted to fame.

Unlike most California mountain lions, which live in large areas of wilderness, P-22 settled in Los Angeles' urban Griffith Park, within view of the famous Hollywood sign. "Discovered" when a remote wildlife camera snapped his picture, P-22's daring *cat*titude quickly attracted a faithful fan following.

Of course, like most celebrities, P-22 is usually elusive. However, wildlife rangers were able to carefully catch and sedate the 120-pound (54-kg) cat, fit him with a tracking collar, and release him back into the wild. Now fans can track his every move! The cool cat even snagged a feature in *National Geographic* magazine.

P-22's fame has grown by leaps and bounds. He's starred in a documentary, and the city of Los Angeles even declared a day of recognition in his honor. Best of all, P-22's fame is raising awareness of mountain lions and the ways that people can peacefully coexist with them.

Great job, P-22—that's a wrap!

Mom, I packed too much. Will you carry my trunk?

Well, they don't call us *PACK*-YDERMS for nothing!

Sometimes Dally takes **NAPS** on Spanky's back.

Dally holds on to Spanky with her paws.

Dog Rides Horse

We're no ONE-TRICK ponies!

SADDLE UP FOR A WILD RIDE with this dynamic duo that really loves to horse around. Dally the dog and Spanky the miniature horse love to hang out, eat together, and go for horseback rides—or at least, Dally goes for a ride on Spanky's back!

This dog-and-pony show began shortly after their owner, Francesca, adopted Spanky. At first, Spanky was a bit of a grouch and didn't like people or other animals. But Dally, a tiny Jack Russell terrier, soon befriended the horse. One day, while they were relaxing in Spanky's pasture, courageous Dally hopped onto the horse's back—all on her own! From then on, riding became their *mane* event.

Dally and Spanky are the **STARS** of a picture book and a coloring book.

Jack Russell terriers were originally bred as **HUNTING DOGS.**

Now, when they're not napping or snacking, the furry friends appear on television and at live events. Dally holds on to Spanky with her paws as he jumps over hurdles and trots around the ring. Giddyup, *paw*tners!

Ember tried too **hard** to **avoid** Mondays.

49

SKUNK HANDSTANDS

IF YOU SEE A SPOTTED SKUNK EXECUTE A PERFECT HANDSTAND, you might think it is hoping to qualify for the floor exercise at the Olympics. These sporty stinkers can walk around on their front paws better than some gymnasts. Give that skunk a perfect 10!

But wait—don't be drawn in by this curious behavior. A skunk doing a handstand means "Back off!" While it's impressive to us humans, the spotted skunk's acrobatic display serves a purpose: It warns predators away and helps the skunk defend itself—really! Standing on its front legs allows the skunk to more than triple its height, creating an intimidating sight that helps deter hungry animals. But if that isn't enough to scare off a predator, the handstand also puts the skunk's tail in perfect position for spraying!

Skunks sometimes **EAT** live honey-bees.

Spotted skunk spray is so potent that it can knock out, or even kill, a predator. Talk about silent but deadly!

All we can say is that if human handstands were like a skunk's, gymnastics would be very different!

TA-DA!

Spotted **SKUNKS** are generally smaller and faster than striped skunks.

Skunks can **SPRAY** as far as 10 feet (3 m).

ANIMAL:

Tokay gecko

NAME:

Crazy Cosmo

FAVORITE DANCE:

The polka (dot)

FAVORITE SAYING:

"I rep the reptiles at *all* the dances!"

The cat flinched

when the finch winced.

53

Mari the **sloth** loves seeing things from **new** points of **view.**

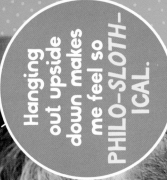

Hanging out upside down makes me feel so PHILO–SLOTH–ICAL.

Jerome hoped his **new disguise** made him completely **anony-*moose*.**

Do you like my *MOOSE-STACHE?*

A. A. Milne named

POOH'S FRIENDS

after his son's stuffed animals.

Pooh and friends enjoy a day in their home, the Hundred Acre Wood.

CRITTER
COMEDIANS

Winnie-the-Pooh

MMM, HONEY. Would you climb a tree for it? Battle bees? Get stuck in a honey pot?! Well, Pooh would!

A sweet, honey-loving bear, Winnie-the-Pooh was created almost a century ago by author A. A. Milne and was inspired by a real-life bear. Since then, Pooh has starred in books, television shows, movies, and more ... but he still can't quite control himself when it comes to golden, sticky, delicious honey—or "hunny," as he calls it! Whether he's getting himself stuck in tight places, badgered by buzzing bees, or just plain lost, this silly old bear will never give up.

Fortunately, when he finds himself in a tizzy, Pooh has a brave band of pals ready to help and join in on the adventures. There's tiny Piglet, who will always overcome his fears to help a friend in need; Pooh's energetic partner-in-crime Tigger; the (mostly) wise Owl; and so many more!

Though Pooh may have a nose for trouble, his good-natured demeanor, can-do spirit, and fantastic friends help him wiggle his backside out of any sticky situation—sometimes even with a face covered in hunny!

TONGUE TWISTERS

The buffalo bounded through the bungalow.

Honestly, I get photobombed in *EVERY* picture!

Dog Becomes Mayor

First on the agenda: **BELLY RUBS!**

Brynn **BECAME MAYOR** after Lucy Lou, a border collie, retired from the position.

RABBIT HASH GENERAL STORE

IN THE TOWN OF RABBIT HASH, KENTUCKY, U.S.A., dogs rule and humans drool.

At least, it's easy to get that idea once you meet the mayor—a five-year-old dog named Brynneth Pawltro! Brynneth, a pit bull, became the town's top dog when she was first elected honorary mayor in 2017. Brynneth—or Brynn for short—was elected as part of a traditional fund-raiser in which residents of the small town donate a dollar to vote for their next mayor. This particular election managed to raise more than $8,000, largely thanks to Brynn—the very good girl won in a landslide, beating contestants that included a cat and a donkey!

According to the residents of Rabbit Hash, Brynn takes her job in *paw*-ffice very seriously. Locals say that she greets visitors and loves children, and according to her owner, Brynn pledges not to chase cats. Luckily for this hardworking hound, being mayor isn't all business. The political pup loves to attend local festivals and soak up the sun—and, of course, get lots of treats and petting!

THE **OWL** THOUGHT HER **JOKES** WERE A **HOOT.**

OWL always love puns!

What kind of sandals do frogs wear?

Crocs?

Open-*TOAD* shoes!

65

ARCHERFISH:
SECRET AGENT?

IMAGINE YOU'RE A BUG, just sitting above the water on a branch minding your own business. Suddenly—*thoomp*—you're struck by a missile launched from underwater! A submarine? No, it's the underwater James Bond, the archerfish.

True to its name (and its aim!), the archerfish shoots "arrows" of water at its prey, knocking its hapless targets from branches or leaves and into the water below. The fish itself remains unseen underwater, as hidden as a secret agent, until it closes in on its stunned prey wriggling on the water's surface.

Amazingly, an archerfish is able to control the speed of a water missile by how quickly or slowly it closes its mouth. In fact, some scientists even consider the way an archerfish manipulates water the same as using a tool.

What kind of tool? One fit for a secret agent, of course!

Archerfish **EAT SPIDERS,** insects, and even small lizards.

Archerfish can pick off **PREY** up to 6 feet (2 m) away.

They call me **FISH.** ARCHERFISH.

ANIMAL:

Cat

NAME:

Daisy

FAVORITE GAME:

Hide-and-seek

FAVORITE SAYING:

"Bet you can't find me!"

SHHH, I'm counting zebras.

The **king** of the jungle doesn't seem so tough when he's just *lion* around.

Bugs Bunny has a star on the **HOLLYWOOD WALK OF FAME.**

Voice actor Mel Blanc ate **CARROTS** while voicing Bugs to accurately create a munching sound.

Bugs Bunny was created by Leon Schlesinger in the 1930s.

BUGS BUNNY, the wisecracking rabbit, is known for always having a hop up on everything and everyone around him. While he'd rather live a quiet life in his burrow, he has no problem popping out to torment Elmer Fudd, even when Fudd is hunting "wabbits" like Bugs!

Whether he's making a fool of Fudd by pulling his cap over his eyes, dropping his drawers, or tying the barrel of his gun into a bow, Bugs always manages to outsmart the hunter and have fun doing it. Some of his most ingenious disguises include a fashionable woman, an old lady, and a variety of celebrities. But his favorite might be that old standby, the barber. It seems Bugs' adversaries, from Elmer Fudd to the Tasmanian Devil to spooky monsters, can't resist popping in for a quick trim— even in the middle of a chase.

Bugs has been up to his antics for more than 70 years! In that time, he's also starred in multiple movies and television shows, won awards, and learned to play multiple instruments, from the piano to the harp. We're sure that Bugs will be asking "Eh ... what's up, doc?" for many years to come.

72

73

Surprise
CAT–TACK!

MITTENS WAS CERTAIN SHE'D BECOME THE **MEOWSTER** OF ALL NINJAS.

75

Favorite books in the animal kingdom:

BEARY PAWTER and the Roarder of the Phoenix
by J.K. Growling

ROMEOW AND MEWLIET
by Shakespurr

DIARY OF A SHRIMPY KID
by Jeff Finney

THE THREE MOUSEKETEERS
by Alexandre Dupaw

Blech, what is that *FOWL* smell?

BIZARRE BEHAVIORS

THE BICHON
BUZZ

IF YOU EVER VISIT SOMEONE'S HOME and happen to encounter a little white blur suddenly darting out of nowhere and zigzagging all around the room, stay calm.

Chances are it's not a cool new toy but a bichon frise, a cheerful, fluffy dog with a fun-loving personality and energy to burn. Bichons love belly rubs and trips to the park like any other dog, but when they get excited—buzz time!—they sprint around and run amok like low-flying drones gone haywire.

Bichons were once a **SYMBOL OF ROYALTY** and nobility in Italy.

Once the buzz—sometimes called the Bichon Blitz—hits, bichons are like tightly coiled windup toys. Darting back and forth at top speed, growling or barking, and stopping to play, these friendly dogs love it when their human companions take part in the fun.

One of these episodes can last up to five minutes, or longer if there is more than one dog in the room. Like any windup or battery-powered toy, the pooch will slow down eventually, but unlike any toy, a bichon will lick your face when the playing session is over. *Awww!*

Bichons are one of the few **DOG BREEDS** that don't shed.

79

Want
to come
hiking?
ALPACA
lunch!

ANIMAL:

Pomeranian

NAME:

Patience

FAVORITE HOLIDAY:

Thanksgiving

FAVORITE SAYING:

"Is it turkey time yet?"

BELLY FLOP!

Pig Paints Pictures

WHEN YOU THINK OF A PAINTING PIG, what do you imagine? An artistic oinker plopping her big pig body down into puddles of mud? For Pigcasso the pig, the process is a little more refined.

Pigcasso was rescued by her owner, Joanne Lefson, in Cape Town, South Africa. Since pigs are intelligent creatures, Joanne hoped to find a fun activity to keep the sweet swine from getting bored. And by using treats and a training tool called a clicker, Joanne was able to teach Pigcasso to paint! Pigcasso simply holds the brush in her mouth, dips it in paint, and gets to work creating masterpieces.

Now, Pigcasso's artwork gets tons of attention. The paintings are even raising money for charity!

So, how do you know you've gotten hold of a Pigcasso original? She "signs" each piece with her noseprint!

Pigcasso loves
CARAMEL POPCORN
and syrup peaches.

Pigcasso even has her own **POP-UP** art exhibition!

Pigcasso paints a landscape.

Pigcasso's art may be delicate, but she **WEIGHS 450 POUNDS** (204 kg).

I majored in business—
MONKEY BUSINESS.

Real animal species names you'll love if you're a witch or wizard:

AMPULEX DEMENTOR

ERIOVIXIA GRYFFINDORI

DRACOREX HOGWARTSIA

HARRYPLAX SEVERUS

CLEVOSAURUS SECTUMSEMPER

AGRA CADABRA

CRITTER COMEDIANS
Lil BUB

BIG EYES? CHECK. A pink tongue that sticks out? Check. Short, stubby legs? Check. Lil BUB has everything she needs to be adorably silly, and so much more!

This fantastically famous feline is beloved by fans all over the globe, but it wasn't always this way. BUB was born with several conditions that make it so she will always look like a tiny kitten, even as she grows older. BUB also has something known as feline dwarfism, which means that her legs are very short compared to the rest of her body. Luckily, BUB was taken in and cared for, and she eventually found a home with someone who knew that her conditions just made her extra special.

In fact, BUB's unique look and sunny outlook on life soon captivated fans from all over! Now BUB spends her time inspiring others to be themselves ... and, of course, to be silly. BUB loves mugging for the camera, whether she's getting baths, riding in toy trucks, hiding in a pile of stuffed animals that look just like her, or leaving cookies for Santa. Her silly escapades—and eye-catching looks—encourage fans to celebrate the differences that make everyone unique ... and to laugh!

BUB has raised more than **$300,000** for charity.

BUB has an **EXTRA TOE** on each foot.

Don't even **TRY** to draw me out of my shell!

SAM WAS **A VERY GRUMPY** SEA TURTLE—AND **HE LIKED IT THAT WAY.**

ANIMAL:

Pug

NAME:

Marco

FAVORITE ACTIVITY:

Long car rides

FAVORITE SAYING:

"Now I get to stick my head out of the window whenever I want!"

CHEERLEADING CRABS!

NEED SOME CHEER? A pom-pom crab will get the job done. The pom-pom crab, also known as the boxer crab, gets its name from—you guessed it—the tiny "pom-poms" it clutches in each claw. But unlike those used by a cheerleader, these pom-poms pack a punch: They are actually anemones! The crabs use these anemones—marine animals with stinging tentacles—to ward off predators and stun prey. (If you've never seen a cheerleader hunt with their pom-poms before, now's your chance!)

And these underwater cheerleaders are also whizzes in the science department. Because anemones are able to grow back lost body parts, the crabs are never left without their best defense (Let's go, defense, let's go!). If a crab ever loses a pom-pom, it simply pulls apart the remaining pom, and voilà—the crab now has two tiny pom-poms that will soon grow back to full size.

Life isn't bad for the anemones, either—after all, the crabs take good care of their pom-poms by feeding them and keeping them safe. Now, that's one team we can root for!

Scientists are not sure how—**OR WHERE**—the crabs get their anemones in the first place.

Give me a
C-R-A-B-S!
What's that spell? Go, crabs!

A **POM-POM CRAB** grows to be only about an inch (2.5 cm) long.

96

MARCELLA:

Why did the fish blush?

TYRONE:

He was escaping a predator?

MARCELLA:

He saw the *OCEAN'S BOTTOM.*

ANIMAL:

Giraffe

NAME:

Genevieve

FAVORITE SPORT:

Boat racing

FAVORITE SAYING:

"I always win—

even when it's neck and neck!"

The orangutan opted to order more oranges.

Goats Take Yoga

ITCHING TO TRY YOUR HOOF AT YOGA? Don't worry—you've *goat* this!

In fact, at Goat Yoga in Oregon, U.S.A., you quite literally goat it—as in, you take your yoga class with the help of some seriously cute goats.

When the founder of Goat Yoga, Lainey Morse, welcomed goats onto her farm, she had no idea that it would be the start of something huge. Lainey already knew that the presence of goats could lower stress, and she was a huge fan of using them for animal-assisted therapy. But it was at the suggestion of a friend that Lainey decided to combine the goats' natural penchants for climbing and snuggling with the calm, positive vibes of yoga class. The result was incredible—goats and yoga were a perfect fit!

Now, classes at the farm involve the "aid" of Lainey's goats—many of whom are rescues—as they clamber, nuzzle, and snuggle while you stretch.

Don't live near Oregon? Not to worry—Goat Yoga has inspired classes all over the world. Not *baaad!*

Some researchers think that **YOGA** may be up to 10,000 years old.

103

Kitty-up, *PAW-TNER!*

105

CRITTER COMEDIANS
Kabosu— the face of Doge

WOW, MUCH FUNNY. SO COMEDY! Kabosu was just your average dog—until she unexpectedly became famous worldwide.

Kabosu is the real-life face behind one of the internet's best known memes: Doge. Memes include funny pictures or images that are edited and shared by people online. Featuring a skeptical Shiba Inu surrounded by grammatically incorrect sayings, this particular meme spread like wildfire, delighting internet aficionados around the world. But at first, Kabosu—and her owner—had no idea this was happening!

Kabosu and her owner, Atsuko Sato, live in Japan. Atsuko had rescued Kabosu from a puppy mill, and she enjoyed sharing pictures of the pup over social media. One day, a friend shared a funny Doge meme with Atsuko, and she realized it was her very own Shiba Inu—Kabosu! Someone on the internet had seen Kabosu's adorable photos, fallen in love with the iconic image people know today, and *poof*—Doge was born. And in addition to appearing everywhere, the meme also gave rise to the popularity of Shiba Inus ... or shibes, as the internet likes to call them.

Today, memes come and go faster than ever, but no one will ever forget Doge—or Kabosu!

Kabosu is named after a type of **JAPANESE FRUIT.**

Kabosu and Atsuko spend their time helping other **SHELTER ANIMALS.**

Most people use the font **COMIC SANS** in their Doge memes.

107

ANIMAL:

Giant panda

NAME:

Tyson

FAVORITE SPORT:

Tennis

FAVORITE SAYING:

"This sport is *panda*-monium!"

Oh my, what a *KOALA-TY* view!

MOTH LOOKS LIKE
BIRD POOP

AH, NATURE. Full of beauty and grace and—wait a minute, is that pile of bird poop moving? Hey, that's no pile of droppings, that's a moth!

Hearing that you look like doo-doo is not usually a compliment, but for the beautiful wood nymph moth, looking like poo may be what keeps it alive.

How? Well, just imagine that you're a hungry bird searching for a snack. There on a leaf, you spot what appears to be bird droppings. Want to take a bite? No way!

Exactly—most animals feel the same way and avoid the cleverly camouflaged beautiful wood nymph. When not disguised, the moth's patterns are striking, and they help attract mates. However, these markings also look delicious to hungry insectivores. But at rest, the moth takes on another—less appetizing—shape entirely, and predators tend to pass it over for a much nicer-looking meal.

So while the beautiful wood nymph may not always be, well, beautiful, it probably wouldn't have it any other way!

Just don't call me a **PARTY POOPER!**

Beautiful **WOOD NYMPHS** live mostly in the eastern United States.

Many species of **MOTHS** do not have mouths.

I spend all my time *SURFING* the web!

113

Fowl Fashion Show

WHAT COULD BE MORE ELEGANT THAN A GOOSE?
A goose on a runway, you say? Nailed it!

At the Pied Piper Duck Show in Sydney, Australia, ducks and geese strut their stuff while wearing outrageous outfits. The show was started by farmer Brian Harrington as part of the Sydney Royal Easter Show and quickly became an annual tradition. Now more than 900,000 people flock to the parade each year to gawk at these fine feathered models.

During the show, participants waddle down a miniature catwalk to cheers. Their outfits often feature fabulous gowns, historical costumes, high-necked attire (of course), and even bride and groom outfits! To top it all off, the ducks finish by racing in their outfits.

Whether or not you're a fan of fashion, these wacky getups are sure to crack you up!

The **PIED PIPER DUCK SHOW** has run for more than 30 years.

A group of geese is called a **GANDER.**

Geese and ducks strut their stuff
at the Pied Piper Duck Show.

Who's up for a game of *DUCK, DUCK, GOOSE?*

DUNG, *Sweet* DUNG

There are more than **8,000 SPECIES** of dung beetles worldwide.

The **ANCIENT EGYPTIANS** revered dung beetles.

YOU HAVE A LOVELY HOME!

FOR THE MIGHTY DUNG BEETLE, there's no place like poo. Dung beetles live in dung (a fancy word for poop), raise their young in it, and even eat it. Some dung beetles roll the manure into balls and cart it away before burying it. Others live directly on top of the waste, and still others tunnel into the droppings. *Ewww,* but true!

Because animals don't digest their food completely, nutritious bits come out in their waste. This sustains the beetles. Many of the beetles prefer herbivore poop, though some seek out omnivore droppings to find juicy bits of meat.

Blech! Just be sure to say "No thanks" if a dung beetle ever rolls out the welcome carpet for you.

Dung beetles can live up to **THREE YEARS.**

A dung beetle uses its strong legs to roll dung into a ball.

FORMAL WEAR WAS **REQUIRED** FOR THE ANNUAL **PENGUIN BALL.**

NO TUXEDO? That just won't fly!

Chickens **DREAM** when they sleep.

Hen Pampers Pups

"**WOOF!**"

WHAT DO YOU GET when you cross a chicken with some puppies? Why, that's Mabel the hen and her barking brood!

After an accident with a horse, Mabel was moved indoors to keep her warm and happy during the winter. However, no one could have predicted just how well she'd take to her new surroundings! In fact, when Nettle the dog had a litter of puppies, Mabel found her true calling: pooch babysitter.

It began suddenly: One day when Nettle slipped away for a break, she and her owners came back to find Mabel perched atop the pups! She was roosting on top of them as she would her own chicks, using her fluffy feathers to keep them warm and cozy.

But this wasn't a one-time event—from then on, whenever Nettle was gone, Mabel took over as the pups' temporary caregiver. Perhaps one day Mabel will have her own brood of chicks to care for, but until then, Nettle and the puppies are lucky to have such an *eggs*-ellent babysitter!

There are roughly **25 BILLION** chickens on the planet—more than any other bird.

TONGUE TWISTERS

The kitten was smitten with mittens.

125

Kermit has appeared in more than 20 **MOVIES**.

Kermit the Frog was first made from an **OLD GREEN COAT**.

Kermit was not the original **STAR** of *The Muppet Show*.

Kermit hangs out with pals Miss Piggy, Gonzo, and Fozzie Bear.

Kermit the Frog

THOUGH HE CLAIMS "It ain't easy being green," the multitalented Kermit the Frog has managed to make quite the life for his gangly green self!

Kermit first appeared on the Hollywood scene in 1955, but he rose to fame as a reporter on the debut of *Sesame Street* in 1969. From there, his star power only grew on *The Muppet Show* in the 1970s, and it is still going strong today. Of course, Kermit is occasionally (OK, often) upstaged by his costars, such as temperamental Miss Piggy, silly Fozzie Bear, or chaos-causing Gonzo. Kermit tries to keep his cool, but when the chaos becomes too much, he flails his arms and yells—just causing us to laugh harder!

Even today, Kermit stars in TV shows and movies (and, of course, in memes). In fact, Kermit is such a superstar, we think it might be a little bit easy being green!

AMUSING ANIMALS

ANIMAL:
Red panda

NAME:
Mei

FAVORITE SPORT:
Surfing

FAVORITE SAYING:
"Hang twenty!"

PEOPLE CALL **THE OCEAN** THE
"ALIEN DEEP"
FOR **GOOD REASON** ...

Dog Eats From High Chair

MAYBE YOU THINK YOU'VE SEEN IT ALL when it comes to pampered pooches—you've seen dogs wearing bow ties, canines in coats, and even hounds with fancy hairstyles. What more could there be? Tons more, as it turns out—just check out Tink, who eats from her very own high chair!

TINK'S condition is called megaesophagus.

Tink, a silver Labrador retriever, has a rare digestive disorder that makes it difficult for food to move from her mouth all the way down to her stomach. This means that Tink has to eat sitting upright so that gravity can do its thing and help get those delicious morsels into her belly. Luckily for Tink, her owner, Tom Sullivan, would stop at nothing to get the precious pup what she needs. Tom turned to the internet for help, and soon a crowd of dog-loving Good Samaritans had donated the funds for a special doggy high chair.

A dog high chair is also called a **BAILEY CHAIR.**

But the pampering doesn't stop there—Tink also has to be burped like a human baby! So, after every meal, she is picked up and gently massaged to ensure that all of her food digests properly.

When she's not chowing down in her chair, Tink has a completely normal doggy life and often hams it up for her fans online. Best of all, she is helping to raise awareness for other dogs with special needs, and proving that pups with unique conditions can lead full and healthy lives.

Tink feels right at home in her chair.

Like most
LABRADORS,
Tink loves the water!

DAD, STOP! That was a food truck tipped over back there!

133

THE ALLURE OF THE
ANGLERFISH

DOWN IN THE DARK AT THE BOTTOM OF THE SEA,
something lurks. "Hee hee, that's right, little sea creatures,
swim right to my jaws—uh, I mean the pretty, totally safe
light..." CHOMP!

Meet the anglerfish, a deep-sea creature with a delightfully
devilish way of luring its food to come to it! Anglerfish have
bulbous eyes, protruding jaws, and, well, faces that
only their mothers could love. So how do these
unique-looking fish attract their fresh sushi
dinners? By luring them with a light. A female
anglerfish, in addition to her great looks, also
has a flowing piece of flesh that dangles from
her head. Because the depths of the ocean are so
dark, most creatures are naturally attracted to this light.

By the time its prey gets close enough to the light, GULP,
the nightmarish mouth of the anglerfish is swallowing it
whole. Drat!

Male
anglerfish are
SMALL—
no bigger than
a finger!

OPEN
24
HOURS

EAT
HERE!

★ ★ ☆

SEA
CREATURES
welcome

SWIM IN!

...FOOD
...taurant

...PINK ☆

There
are more than
200
DIFFERENT
known species of
anglerfish.

My
favorite is the
**SEAFOOD
SPECIAL.**

The intelligent elephant was equally elegant.

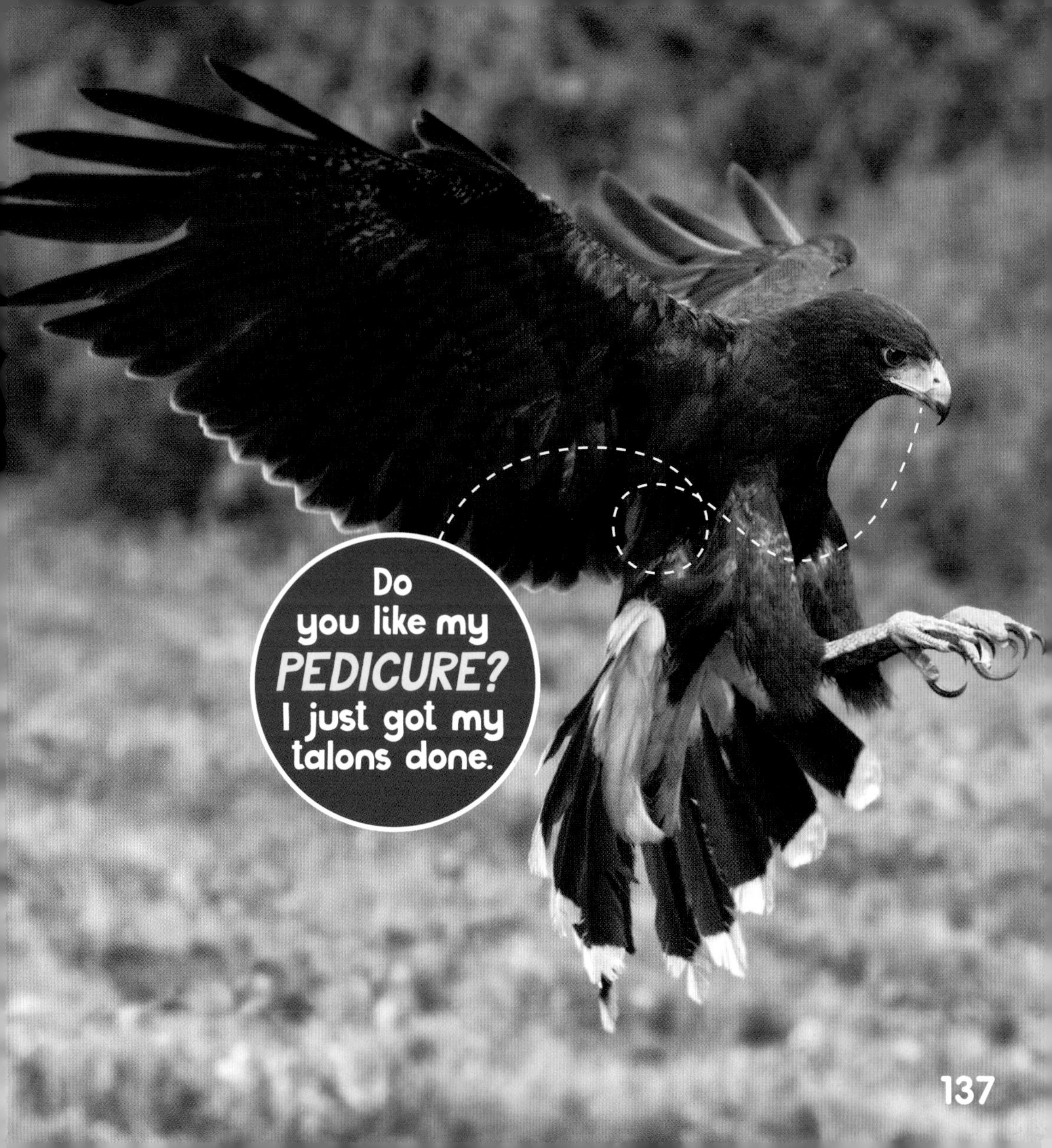
Do
you like my
PEDICURE?
I just got my
talons done.

Pierre was a surprisingly **great dancer:** His special was the **toucan-can.**

I always aim for **BEAK** performance in my dances!

AMUSING ANIMALS

ANIMAL:

Chihuahua

NAME:

Pistol Paige

JOB:

Sheriff of Dog Town

FAVORITE SAYING:

"When the goin' gets *ruff*,
the *ruff* get goin.'"

What do you call a black-and-blue mark on a brontosaurus?

A bruise?

A DINO-SORE.

Doggy Surf-A-Thon

TOTALLY GNARLY!

Past events have raised more than **$80,000** for homeless animals!

AT A SURFING CONTEST IN DEL MAR, CALIFORNIA, U.S.A., the contestants are experts at the dog paddle—because the surfers are all dogs!

Held annually by a nonprofit animal rescue organization called the Helen Woodward Animal Center, the Surf Dog Surf-A-Thon lets pup participants catch waves instead of balls. Pooches of all shapes and sizes line up to "hang twenty," perching on special soft surfboards and riding the waves in to shore. *Pawticipants* can also join in on a costume contest, a dog agility course, and plenty of music, food, and fun! Best of all, the event raises awareness and money for homeless animals.

Cowabunga—er, *dogabunga!*

Every dog wears a special **LIFE VEST** to stay safe.

Sealia swore she could see the sea.

COWS CHOW
IN ONE DIRECTION

IMAGINE IT'S A NORMAL SCHOOL DAY. You've made it through morning classes and are excited to grab some grub. But when you head to the cafeteria, you notice something strange ... All your classmates seem to be ... eating facing one direction? What's going on? For cows, this is normal behavior.

A team at a university in Germany discovered something pretty strange: While eating or resting, all cows in a pasture faced the same direction, either due north or due south. The researchers found that cows are highly influenced by the natural magnetism—or should we say *moo*gnetism—of our planet's North and South Poles.

Scientists are still theorizing about why this happens. Is it a leftover instinct from when cows roamed freely in herds? Or do they have a cosmic connection with alien forces that we simple humans just haven't recognized yet? (OK, it's probably the first one.)

Experts plan on running more tests. In the meantime, if you ever get lost outdoors without a smartphone, just find the nearest dairy pasture and use the *cow*mpass!

A male cow, called a **BULL,** can weigh up to 2,400 pounds (1,089 kg)!

We **MOOOVE** together!

Cows can see almost **360** DEGREES around themselves.

Animal groups that would make great metal bands:

CAULDRON OF BATS

MURDER OF CROWS

KNOT OF TOADS

SHIVER OF SHARKS

TRIBE OF GOATS

QUIVER OF COBRAS

KETTLE OF HAWKS

Don't
be jealous
just because I'm
**WOOLLY
COOL.**

149

SHH, don't tell the chicken.

BESSIE WANTED TO BE THE NEXT BIG COMEDY STAR.

150

153

UGH, school lice checks are the worst.

The sea slug shook the sugar.

AAH, naps are always cozy when you come with your own fur blanket!

157

Hippos can spend up to **16 HOURS** a day in the water.

Fiona weighed only **29 POUNDS** (13 kg) when she was born.

Fiona poses for the camera with her mom.

CRITTER COMEDIANS
Fiona the Hippo

WHO'S THE HOTTEST new star at the zoo? A polar bear? Please. A lion? No way! The newest animal sensation is none other than Fiona the hippo!

Fiona was born at the Cincinnati Zoo in Ohio, U.S.A., six weeks early, so she was too small and weak to be cared for by her mother. The zoo staff was able to give Fiona around-the-clock care. This included feeding her from a bottle, giving her baths, and teaching her to walk. They documented Fiona's progress on social media, and she became a sensation! Fans loved Fiona's determination and her silly expressions.

Soon people from all over were making trips to the Cincinnati Zoo to see their favorite celebrity. Crowds went wild over Fiona's sassy attitude toward her parents and her adorable underwater hippo rolls. People even loved it when she tooted! The zoo staff eventually created an online show for Fiona, called *The Fiona Show*.

Whether she is an icon, as some fans say, or a diva, one thing is for sure—she's a star. Keep spreading the love and laughs, Fiona!

One couple got **ENGAGED** while Fiona looked on!

ANIMAL:

Rabbit

NAME:

Chef Pierre le Hare

FAVORITE SHOW:

Hop Chef

FAVORITE SAYING:

"You might call it rabbit food, but I call it gourmet!"

None may enter the blanket fort of Captain Fluffy Whiskerkins!

KANGAROOS BOXXX

LADIES AND GENTLEMEN, step right up to nature's greatest boxing match! In one corner, standing six feet (2 m) tall and weighing in at 200 pounds (91 kg), is a kangaroo! And in the other corner, all the way from down under, we have ... another kangaroo?

Yes, it's true, male kangaroos really do "box." When two male kangaroos, called boomers, come into conflict—usually over a mate—they duke it out. But unlike in professional boxing, there are no rules. Boomers use their arms and paws to bop each other, but they also use their incredibly powerful legs to kick! And, of course, there's no referee to call a time-out.

Even baby kangaroos, called joeys, box! Joeys, however, are just playing—and their boxing is way more adorable.

So which kangaroo are you kanga-rooting for?

Kangaroos can cover **25 FEET** (8 m) in a single bound.

Hop to it, *MATE!*

Newborn **JOEYS** are just an inch (2.5 cm) long—about the size of a grape.

164

How **DARE** you eat that last fry in front of me!

In addition to **LASAGNA,** Garfield loves sandwiches, coffee, and doughnuts.

Garfield and Odie go for a wild ride.

CRITTER
COMEDIANS

Garfield the Cat

DID YOU KNOW THAT the original Grumpy Cat made his debut in a newspaper comic strip in 1978?

You probably know him as Garfield, the lasagna-loving, Monday-hating feline. Garfield was born in an Italian restaurant but was given away after eating too much pasta. He'd clean out all the Italian restaurants in town, with the resulting belch reportedly bellowing all the way into the next borough.

Luckily for Garfield, he was rescued by his new owner, Jon Arbuckle. Unluckily for Jon, he didn't quite know what he was getting himself into! Garfield has turned out to be quite the *pawful*, from eating Jon's food and stealing his newspapers to pranking the gullible but lovable dog Odie. Garfield has even let a group of mice take up residence in Jon's house, refusing to chase them because it is just too much work.

But annoy Jon as they might, Garfield's actions never fail to make us laugh. Stay grumpy, Garfield!

Garfield is a **TABBY**, which refers to his striped coat.

Ways animals say "Happy Birthday":

Have a **TWEET** bird-day!

Somebunny wants to say **HOPPY** birthday!

Happy **BEE-DAY!**

Happy **PURR-thday!**

PUPPY birthday!

Cat Burglar Snatches Clothes

WAKING UP AND FINDING OUT YOU'VE BEEN ROBBED IS NO FUN, and when you find out the thief stole your underpants—well, that just stinks!

For one town, though, this is a common occurrence. You could say they suffer from a local cat burglar—literally! In Hamilton, New Zealand, no one's unmentionables are safe from Brigit the cat.

Brigit once brought home a **HOCKEY SHIN PAD!**

It all began when Brigit's owner, Sarah Nathan, started noticing extra clothing in the laundry. Some socks here, some unfamiliar underwear there—what was going on? Sarah did some sleuthing and discovered that the culprit was none other than Brigit, her Tonkinese cat! It seemed that Brigit was sneaking off to swipe clothing from the neighbors' clotheslines, returning only to deposit her prizes at Sarah's front door.

Hoping to return the—ahem—delicates to their rightful owners, Sarah handed out flyers about the missing items. She even made a post on social media and was shocked when it went viral! It seems that no one can stay angry at such a cute thief.

Luckily for the residents of Hamilton, Sarah and her family plan to move to the countryside, which will likely put an end to Brigit's pilfering ways. Until then—guard your drawers!

Brigit shows off her many spoils.

It's the
PURRFECT
crime!

Brigit has stolen more than 11 pairs of underwear and

50 PAIRS OF SOCKS.

AMUSING ANIMALS

ANIMAL:

Little owl

NAME:

Ajay

FAVORITE HOBBY:

Traveling the world

FAVORITE SAYING:

"Owl see you soon!"

AAH, THAT **MEWMENT** WHEN YOU REALIZE IT'S **THE WEEKEND!**

Destiny couldn't figure out why the other **animals** kept **running** away.

This isn't what I was expecting when they said they hired a new dog walker!

CHO:
What do you call an alligator wearing a vest and looking for clues?

MARI:
Fancy?

CHO:
An in-vest-i-GATOR.

177

BIZARRE
BEHAVIORS

MASTER OF DISGUISE

WHO DO YOU THINK OF AS A MASTER OF DISGUISE?

A famous spy? A superhero with amazing powers? ... An octopus?

Just like a secret agent or a comic book character, the mimic octopus can resemble almost anything—from a crab to a lionfish to a jellyfish! While it will typically copy the colors of the environment it's in, it can also shift shape to turn the tables on potential predators. In fact, a mimic octopus can "transform" into more than 10 different animals! Talk about a superpower.

Scientists believe that the octopus chooses which animal to mimic based on which predators—or archenemies—are nearby. Some mimics even use their disguises to feed, taking on the form of a crab, and then—*snap!*—gobbling up any prey unlucky enough to be fooled. The mimic deserves a round of applause for bringing its copycat—er, copyoctopus—ways to a new level.

Scientists have discovered a type of fish that **MIMICS** the mimic octopus!

A **MIMIC OCTOPUS** lives for about nine months.

The mimic octopus copies a mantis shrimp.

181

It's
IRR-*ELEPHANT*
that you're a
human; you're
my best
friend!

The **big black bear** bit a **blue bug.**

ANIMAL:

Cat

NAME:

Jack O. Lantern

FAVORITE HOLIDAY:

Halloween

FAVORITE SAYING:

"Trick or treat, smell my feet, give me fish and mice to eat!"

Penguin Becomes a Knight

IT WAS A RAINY MORNING, and Nils Olav II had just been promoted from knight to brigadier. Brigadier Olav walked down the line of attending soldiers, his insignia glistening in the gray light. Unlike most brigadiers, however, Nils is also a king—a king penguin, that is.

AT EASE, SOLDIERS.

Nils Olav II, a king penguin at the Edinburgh Zoo in Scotland, is a knighted honorary member of the King of Norway's Guard. This unlikely honor was originally bestowed on the first Nils Olav back in 1972, when Norway's royal guard first visited the Edinburgh Zoo and decided to adopt a penguin as a mascot. Since then, Nils Olav II has proudly carried on the tradition and is grandly promoted each time the Guard visits.

In addition to looking very formal in his natural penguin tuxedo, Nils dons the brigadier rank insignia on his wing for special occasions. That's Sir King Penguin, to you!

Nils Olav II wears the brigadier insignia on his wing.

KING PENGUINS are the second largest penguin, after emperor penguins.

The **pufferfish** wished she switched dishes.

Oh, did I
MOOOVE
too close?

An **ITCHING BEAR** will sometimes use its front paws to grab another branch for balance.

Now that's what I call a **BEAR** NECESSITY!

ITCHY BEARS

Bears seem to have favorite **"RUB TREES"** and will return to the same one many times.

HAVE YOU EVER HAD AN ITCH IN A REALLY HARD-TO-REACH PLACE?
You stretch and bend, but you just can't seem to scratch the middle of your back. Time to take a tip from ... a bear? You bet. When a bear has an itch that won't quit, does he ask another bear to lend a paw? No! He just finds a nice rough tree and boogies down.

By setting up remote wildlife cameras in the United States and Canada, scientists were able to capture grizzly and black bears shimmying, shaking, and generally getting down while they scratched their itchy behinds on some nice bumpy tree bark. But why? Do they just love a good dance party? Some experts believe that by rubbing their backs, rumps, and faces on trees, the bears are getting rid of their itchy winter coats. Others believe that male bears might do this to mark territory.

Either way, it makes for quite a performance!

Larry, why are we stampeding?
What? I thought we were playing TAG!

Walt Disney originally wanted to call Disneyland **"MICKEY MOUSE VILLAGE."**

Legend has it that Walt Disney was able to **TAME A MOUSE** by feeding it crumbs.

Mickey takes the wheel in this still from "Steamboat Willie."

194

CRITTER COMEDIANS
Mickey Mouse

POSSIBLY THE MOST FAMOUS of all animal comedians, Mickey Mouse is beloved by fans of all ages. Created by Walt Disney, he was the first cartoon character ever to appear in an animated film with sound, in a short called "Steamboat Willie," in 1928. Since then, the marvelous mouse has become known by generations of fans for his wit, charisma, and nose for trouble!

Wait, trouble? Sure, Mickey means well, but his curiosity and forgetfulness often combine in unforgettable ways! When Mickey orders a build-it-yourself airplane kit for a date with Minnie, he rushes through the assembly instructions, and Minnie has to bail them out—literally! And in the classic film *The Sorcerer's Apprentice,* Mickey figures out how to use his master's magic hat to do his janitorial chores ... until a broom takes on a life of its own. Yikes!

Luckily, Mickey's quick thinking always saves the day, along with help from friends Minnie, Donald, Goofy, Pluto, and more.

And really, Mickey can't be *that* bumbling or forgetful—after all, he runs one of the most famous theme parks in the world!

They didn't even **paws** before tearing into their **bear-day** cake!

Where do sharks love to vacation?

Crowded public beaches?

FINLAND.

Bearcats use their **URINE** to mark their territory.

BEARCAT URINE SMELLS LIKE

BUTTERED POPCORN.

Mmm, what's that smell? Popcorn? Nope! Fooled you—it's just *BEARCAT PEE.*

BEARCATS,
ALSO CALLED BINTURONGS,

are neither bears nor cats. Found in Southeast Asia, they are small forest-dwelling mammals with a unique appearance. And bearcats have something else that is unique: their urine! The sweet-smelling creatures have a particular chemical in their pee that gives off the scent of hot, buttered popcorn. The chemical, called 2-AP, is also found in cooked rice and toasted bread. *Mmm!*

Scientists have even conducted research to find out exactly why bearcat pee smells so yummy. (Yes, there are a bunch of scientists in a lab smelling pee samples from wild animals!)

So the next time your mouth starts watering after smelling buttered popcorn, keep these little critters in mind!

A male bearcat's urine is **STINKIER** than a female's.

Stu the gnu chewed through shoes.

Animals you'd find in the bathroom:

DOO-DOO birds

Hip**POOS**

TOOT-cans

STINK bugs

POOdles

CACA-roaches

STINKPOT turtles

Scooby-Doo's full name is **SCOOBERT DOO.**

CRITTER COMEDIANS

Scooby-Doo

IF THERE'S A MYSTERY TO BE SOLVED, don't call Scooby-Doo—unless you have some Scooby Snacks on hand!

Scooby-Doo is a Great Dane with a big heart and an even bigger appetite. He and his friends—Fred Jones, Daphne Blake, Velma Dinkley, and Scooby-Doo's BFF, Shaggy Rogers—make up the crime-solving team known as Mystery, Inc. Together, they come face-to-face with seemingly haunted houses, creepy creatures, and villains in disguise. But in spite of his large size, Scooby-Doo is a bit of a scaredy-cat—er, scaredy-dog—and he and Shaggy would rather turn tail and flee than dive into danger. Luckily, the goofy pair would do anything for delicious Scooby Snacks and are always encouraged to save the day and unmask the monster.

Scooby-Doo and the gang first appeared in the 1969 television series *Scooby-Doo, Where Are You!* and went on to star in multiple series spin-offs, animated films, and even two live-action movies. It's fair to say these "meddling kids" won't be going away anytime soon!

The gang travels in style in a tricked-out van known as the **MYSTERY MACHINE.**

Time for a **round** of **app-***paws!*

CREDITS

Cover (panda), Gary Vestal/Photographer's Choice/GI; (fox), Eric Isselee/SS; (fake nose and glasses [on fox]), nito/SS; (kitten), Tuzemka/SS; back cover (dog), Lauren Pretorius/SS; (library background), BPTU/SS; (mortar cap), Pixfiction/SS; (stack of books), Billion Photos/SS; (monkey), Timothy Knox/IS/GI; 1 (hippos), Jens Goos/SS; 1 (tub), Ttatty/SS; 2 (blowfish), Beth Swanson/SS; 2 (guitar stand), bluebloodbkk/SS; 2 (electric guitar), Yuri Shevtsov/SS; 2 (poodle), Jagodka/SS; 2 (fish), holbox/SS; 3 (gecko), Eric Isselee/SS; 3 (glasses), Tetiana Yurchenko/SS; 3 (spider), Nyvlt-art/SS; 3 (toad), Michiel de Wit/SS; 4, Annette Shaff/SS; 5 (cars), Narong Jongsirikul/SS; 5 (giraffe), Jak Wonderly/NGS; 6-7, Fuzzberta Friends/REX/SS; 8, Lauren Pretorius/SS; 9 (stack of money), Eti Swinford/DS; 9 (lobster), Yellowj/SS; 9 (money in claw), olavs/SS; 10, Dmitry Balakirev/SS; 11, Vincent Grafhorst/MP; 12, Kletr/SS; 13, Photodisc; 14-15, Zelenenka/DS; 15 (mouse), Rudmer Zwerver/SS; 15 (computer on desk), SS/Early Spring; 16, Peter Reijners/SS; 17 (penguin), Dmytro Pylypenko/SS; 17 (grass and soccer ball), BK foto/SS; 17 (whistle), FabrikaSimf/SS; 18, April Hamlin/WeRunRace Photos; 19 (LE), Gregg Gelmis/WeRunRacePhotos; 19 (CTR), Jake Armstrong/WeRunRace Photos; 19 (RT), Gregg Gelmis/WeRunRacePhotos; 20, wim claes/SS; 21, Vitaly Titov & Maria Sidelnikova/SS; 21 (BACK), Socrates/DS; 22-23, Derek Liu & Laine Lee/Haus of Waffles; 24 (moth), James Laurie/SS; 24, Janossy Gergely/SS; 25, Ed Samuel/SS; 27 (ferret on hind legs), Eric Isselee/SS; 27 (white ferret standing), Jagodka/SS; 27 (top hat), Gemenacom/SS; 27 (tutu), Inna Zueva Nikolaevna/SS; 28, Vikulin/SS; 29, steveball/SS; 30-31, Tom Gray; 32, Heini Wehrle/BIA/MP; 33, Smit/SS; 34-35, Gary Bell/oceanwideimages.com; 35 (cowboy hat), dashadima/SS; 35 (sheriff's badge), dashadima/SS; 36, WilleeCole Photog/SS; 36 (spots on floor), webmaster7/SS; 37, Dennis Von Linden/SS; 38-39, Steve Jenkins; 40, Sari ONeal/SS; 41, Tim Gainey/AL; 42, Steve Winter/National Geographic Creative; 43 (UP LE), Uncredited/AP/SS; 43 (UP CTR), Steve Winter/National Geographic Creative; 43 (UP RT), Miguel Ordenana; 43 (CTR LE), National Park Service; 43 (CTR RT), Miguel Ordenana; 43 (LO LE), Miguel Ordenana; 43 (LO RT), Uncredited/AP/SS; 44, Cor Meenderinck/SS; 45 (BACK), Johannes Kornelius/SS; 45 (dog), Eric Isselee/SS; 46-47, Isobel Springett; 48, Donald M. Jones/MP; 49 (seagull), Robert Sholl/DS; 49 (bagel), Binh Thanh Bui/SS; 50 (skunk), Jay Pierstorff/SS; 50 (bees), Vinicius Tupinamba/SS; 51, John Downer Productions/Nature Picture Library; 52 (gecko), Eric Isselee/SS; 52 (glasses), Tetiana Yurchenko/SS; 52 (BACK), Egor Tetiushev/SS; 53 (cat), nevodka/SS; 53 (bird), cynoclub/SS; 54-55, Cuson/SS; 56 (spider from above), Nyvlt-art/SS; 56, (spiderweb) Henrik Larsson/SS; 56 (laptop), artjazz/SS; 56 (spider from side), Akil Rolle-Rowan/SS; 56 (spider from front), aSuruwataRi/SS; 57, Green Mountain Exposure/SS; 57 (mustache), Mikhail Grachikov/SS; 58, Moviestore collection Ltd/AL; 59, AF archive/AL; 60 (buffalo), Eric Isselee/SS; 60 (bungalow), pics721/SS; 61, Shadowmac Photography/SS; 62-63, Jordan Bamforth; 63 (sign), Liane Harrold/AL; 64, James Pintar/SS; 65 (alligator) Robert Eastman/SS; 65 (top frog), Adam Gryko/SS; 65 (bottom frog), Hintau Aliaksei/SS; 66-67, Kim Taylor/Nature Picture Library; 68 (stuffed animals), Pixavril/SS; 68 (kitten in frog costume), Annette Shaff/SS; 69, kongsak sumano/SS; 70, United Archives GmbH/AL; 71, Moviestore/REX/SS; 72 (brown bear), Vishnevskiy Vasil/SS; 72 (gummy bears), Surasak Klinmontha/SS; 73, ZSSD/MP; 74-75, sduben/SS; 76 (book), Jiri Hera/SS; 76 (castle), nusfish/SS; 76 (grizzly bear), Scott E Read/SS; 76 (eye glasses), Creative_Stockphoto/SS; 76 (striped scarf), Chekyravaa/SS; 76 (wand), Ruksutakarn studio/SS; 76 (text in book), gnizay/SS; 77, David P. Lewis/SS; 78 (dog), Jacqueline Abromeit/SS; 78 (drone), Sfio Cracho/SS; 78-79 (dog on hind legs), Eudyptula/SS; 79 (windup lever), lucadp/SS; 80, Teno3/SS; 81 (honey badger), Edward Young/SS; 81 (wooden table), EE_Stocker/SS; 81 (menu holder), JoyImage/SS; 81 (red checked napkin), NYS/SS; 82-83, David Thyberg/SS; 83 (binoculars), Soloviova Liudmyla/SS; 83 (helmet), Kletr/SS; 84, Sarah Lew/SS; 84 (BACK), Nick Fox/SS; 85, Paul S. Wolf/SS; 86-87, Joanne Lefson; 88 (BACK), BPTU/SS; 88 (mortar cap), Pixfiction/SS; 88 (monkey), Timothy Knox/IS/GI; 88 (stack of books), Billion Photos/SS; 89, Maya Kruchankova/SS; 90-91, Mike Bridavsky; 92, abc7/SS; 93 (BACK), olgaru79/SS;

COPYRIGHT

Since 1888, the National Geographic Society has funded more than 12,000 research, exploration, and preservation projects around the world. The Society receives funds from National Geographic Partners, LLC, funded in part by your purchase. A portion of the proceeds from this book supports this vital work. To learn more, visit natgeo.com/info.

For more information, visit nationalgeographic.com, call 1-800-647-5463, or write to the following address:

National Geographic Partners
1145 17th Street N.W.
Washington, D.C. 20036-4688 U.S.A.

Visit us online at nationalgeographic.com/books

For librarians and teachers: ngchildrensbooks.org

More for kids from National Geographic: natgeokids.com

National Geographic Kids magazine inspires children to explore their world with fun yet educational articles on animals, science, nature, and more. Using fresh storytelling and amazing photography, *Nat Geo Kids* shows kids ages 6 to 14 the fascinating truth about the world—and why they should care. **kids.nationalgeographic.com/subscribe**

For information about special discounts for bulk purchases, please contact National Geographic Books Special Sales: specialsales@natgeo.com

For rights or permissions inquiries, please contact National Geographic Books Subsidiary Rights: bookrights@natgeo.com

Designed by Brett Challos

Library of Congress Cataloging-in-Publication Data

Names: National Geographic Kids (Firm), publisher. | National Geographic Society (U.S.)
Title: Funny animals/by National Geographic Kids.
Description: Washington, DC : National Geographic Kids, [2019] | Audience: Ages 8-12. | Audience: Grades 4 to 6. | Includes index.
Identifiers: LCCN 2018031441| ISBN 9781426333088 (pbk.) | ISBN 9781426333095 (hardcover)
Subjects: LCSH: Animals--Humor--Juvenile literature. | Animals--Anecdotes--Juvenile literature. | Animals--Miscellanea--Juvenile literature.
Classification: LCC QL49 .F95 2019 | DDC 590.2/07--dc23
LC record available at https://lccn.loc.gov/2018031441

The publisher would like to thank Mojo Media, author; Paige Towler, project editor and contributing writer; Lori Epstein, photo director; Molly Reid, production editor; and Anne LeongSon and Gus Tello, production assistants.

Printed in China
18/PPS/1